Praise for {#289-128}

"Randall Horton's fourth book moves brilliantly from the confines of a prison cell to the expanse of New York City. As 'state poet #289-128,' Horton vividly evokes the dehumanizing experience of prison and the system that enables it. Racial awareness is implicit: 'skin color / is a race that never stops running,' and prison remains a presence even when the poet is free to ride the subway and chronicle a vibrant array of urban lives. 'Poems need to bite,' he says, and these poems do."—Martha Collins, author of *Because What Else Could I Do*

"There is something about trauma that poetry alone can speak to: it can distill pain and wrench something beautiful from it. Horton's stunning work does just this, laying bare the dehumanizing horrors of prison and transforming them into gorgeous art."—Baz Dreisinger, founding director of the Prison-to-College Pipeline program at City University of New York and author of *Incarceration Nations*

"How easy it is for me to salute inmate #289-128. Perhaps I'm in the visitor's chair imploring to our protagonist why we must endure it all—why the darkness, the case, the 'story of survival no one survives' might be worth it all in the end. How we got here, we kind of know how this happens. But what we must undertake is a gruesome, soul-snatching, blues-collecting, head-to-toe humanity-stripping kind of testifying. How we'll end up, we kind of know—but what's for sure is that Randall Horton is my favorite poet. And his words are my favorite reminder. And this secular preaching is the kind of gospel that makes Etheridge and the underworld gods proud."—Derrick Harriell, author of *Cotton* and *Ropes*

"Horton serves as a cicerone to life behind the walls, guiding us with clear eyes through the cell and the yard, through the mess hall and tiers. He also proves himself a sage, revealing knowing truths about the humans we feed into a carnivorous American carceral system: their doubts and hopes, their wounds, their searches for healing. . . . A necessary voice in these troubled times."—Mitchell S. Jackson, author of *Survival Math*

"Horton turns his gift of musical language toward the contemplative, and we find a world larger than our imaginations. It's hyperreal; it's magical; it's filled with solitude, communion, and truth; but, even more surprising, it's a world behind bars that's all around us. We've just ignored it. . . . {#289-128} also teaches us about relationships during a time when we're paying more attention to both how we talk to one another and, as a result, how we love."—A. Van Jordan, author of *The Cineaste*

"Horton's work is urgent and sensitive. With attention to detail and generosity, he forces us to confront the everyday brutality of the criminal punishment bureaucracy. We must open our hearts and minds to the images he offers us, and then we must dismantle the system."—Alec Karakatsanis, founder of the Civil Rights Corps and author of *Usual Cruelty*

"Horton sketches a face of incarceration that, as the system wills it, appears interchangeable and dismissible to the public eye. But in these pages his collectivized voice becomes a form of power, a force impossible to ignore. . . . Horton's true gift lies in the refusal of neat packaging, in questioning both the possibility and failures of language, routinely turning poetry on its axis to examine: can craft appropriately hold the sheer violence of incarceration? Horton's book is at once a landmine of nuance, and a strong medicine against our country's most oppressive and horrific systems."—Caits Meissner, PEN America Prison and Justice Writing Program Director

"A powerfully evocative collection. . . . To question the story of incarceration is to question the ways in which we too are held captive within coded spaces and social contracts, 'trapped / in a maze of identity & boundaries.' Horton's undaunted lyricism shatters this hall of mirrors with a voice transcendent, challenging us to uncover a deeper empathy within and without bounds, where 'the voiceless are alive, too.'"—Monica Ong, author of *Silent Anatomies*

"This book is not a literati 'been there' selfie; not a cred advertisement. It is not even simply accurate, authentic witness. Take that with the fact that this work is masterfully accomplished and skilled writing, and it becomes clear that *{#289-128}* is the real deal."—Ed Roberson, author of *To See the Earth Before the End of the World*

"Horton, who was himself 'property of the state,' writes about 'the slow fatality of imprisonment' with searing insight. These are his trials, his Passion—a word whose root means suffering. This is a must-read voice for our time 'screaming in a dark ocean'; a voice for all times that reminds us how much is lost when we confine a person's humanity to a number." —Lucinda Roy, author of *Fabric: Poems* and *The Dreambird Chronicles*

"A powerful, bristling, innovative serial poem from the carceral state, the beating heart of a brilliant poet's life inside. This is life as a number, a routine, but with razor perception, elegant stride, and heightened observation of the human. . . . An essential book of poetry of this time, right now. . . . This book is a goad to keep by your side as the world awakens to understand its penal tragedies and advocates a visionary change."—Anne Waldman, author of *Trickster Feminism* and chancellor emeritus of the Academy of American Poets

{#289-128}

{#289-128}

POEMS

RANDALL HORTON

UNIVERSITY PRESS OF KENTUCKY

Scholarly publisher for the Commonwealth,
serving Bellarmine University, Berea College, Centre
College of Kentucky, Eastern Kentucky University,
The Filson Historical Society, Georgetown College,
Kentucky Historical Society, Kentucky State University,
Morehead State University, Murray State University,
Northern Kentucky University, Transylvania University,
University of Kentucky, University of Louisville,
and Western Kentucky University.
All rights reserved.

Editorial and Sales Offices: The University Press of Kentucky
663 South Limestone Street, Lexington, Kentucky 40508-4008
www.kentuckypress.com

Library of Congress Cataloging-in-Publication Data

Names: Horton, Randall, author.
Title: {#289-128} : poems / Randall Horton.
Description: Lexington, Kentucky : University Press of Kentucky, [2020] |
   Series: The University Press of Kentucky new poetry & prose series
Identifiers: LCCN 2020017978 | ISBN 9780813180410 (hardcover ; acid-
free paper) | ISBN 9780813179889 (paperback ; acid-free paper) | ISBN
9780813179896 (pdf) | ISBN 9780813179902 (epub)
Subjects: LCSH: Imprisonment—Poetry. | LCGFT: Poetry.
Classification: LCC PS3608.O7727 A614 2020 | DDC 811/.6—dc23
LC record available at https://lccn.loc.gov/2020017978

This book is printed on acid-free paper meeting
the requirements of the American National Standard
for Permanence in Paper for Printed Library Materials.

Manufactured in the United States of America.

Member of the Association
of University Presses

For Rubie, Álvaro, and Chico

I would like to thank the Poetry Center at
the University of Arizona, the Soze Agency,
and Civil Rights Corps in Washington, DC,
for the grant support that assisted in creating this volume.

Contents

POET IN NEW YORK

{#289-128}

PROPERTY OF THE STATE

*These are not images to cheer you
—except that you may see in these small acts
some evidence of my thought and caring*
                          —Dennis Brutus

: ANIMALS

The only thing less than a nigga is a prisoner.

—Rojai Fentress, August Correctional Center

a heatwave envelops the mid-atlantic
  abnormal like the notion of prison
  outside an unrelenting centigrade
oven bakes the male housing unit—

cells are jam-packed with the guilty
  who pled out though very innocent
  7 sounded better than 25 straight
for more than a few consecutive days

there is a spell cast over the complex
  a 5″ fan oscillates the aroma of piss
  from the toilet bowl & it's jungle-like
where grown men & young boys blend

each inmate's sadness compounded—
  no shade nowhere to hide & running
  will get that ass shot at the razor fence
dangling in blood so you sit—suffer

while asking *is this how the story ends?*

3

: ARREST WARRANT

hereby an order is issued to appear
stand before ethical gatekeepers
failure to comply is not an option

jurors of the common body the state
do believe an illegitimate break a tear
in society's framework did transpire

in violation of article 27 section 30(a)
contrary to the act of assembly against
peace a true bill no one will care about

{#289-128}

criminal {#289-128} shall inherit destiny
underneath a systemic bootheel
no one will bemoan dire circumstance

racism, disparities, unemployment, habit
lack of wealth nor egalitarianism—
the usual roadblocks shall be futile

in this quest to not only detain but yes
ensure erasure transpires for the good.

4

DISTRICT COURT OF MARYLAND FOR Montgomery County
Located at 27 Courthouse Square, Rockville, Maryland 20850

Case No.:005D00079574

STATE OF MARYLAND　　　　　　　VS　　　　**HORTON, RANDALL GAVIN**

COMPLAINANT:
Officer: ▮▮▮▮
Agency/Subagency: MCP G15
ID: 0643

CC#: 99041592　　　SID:
Local ID: 153705　　DL#:　　　　　　　　　　DL State:
Race: I　Sex: M　Height: 5'8"　Weight: 160　Hair: BLK　Eyes: BRN
DOB: 10/16/1960　Phone(H):　　　　　　Phone(W):

CHARGES

UPON THE FACTS CONTAINED IN THE APPLICATION ▮▮▮▮
IT IS FORMALLY CHARGED THAT HORTON, RANDALL GAVIN at
the dates, times ▮▮▮▮ below:

NUM	CHG/CIT	STATUTE	PENALTY
001	2 3010	2730	15 Y

On or About 02/19/1999 - 02/22/1999 at 8:00AM

...did break and enter ▮▮▮▮ with the intent to commit ▮
▮▮▮▮ Art. ▮
Against the Peace, Government, and Dignity of the State.

| 002 | 2 3010 | 2730 | 15 Y |

On or About 02/19/1999 - 02/22/1999 at 8:00AM

...did break and enter ▮▮▮▮ with the intent to commit ▮
▮▮▮▮ Art. ▮
Against the Peace, Government, and Dignity of the State.

| 003 | 2 3010 | 2730 | 15 Y |

On or About 02/19/1999 - 02/22/1999 at 8:00AM

...did break and enter ▮▮▮▮
commit ▮▮▮▮ Art. 27, ▮▮▮▮ with the intent to
Against the Peace, Government, and Dignity of the State.

Date: 04/23/1999　　Time: 12:35 PM　　Judicial Officer:

: DON'T TRUST THE PROCESS

weight & waiting & wait—
naked stand before a guard
you are now quite invisible

will not materialize through
iron nor the ignorant—
nothing changes nothing:

intake, property, medical
seize a piece of humanity
each destination a moral point

converging toward a cell
hidden in the open by a lie
no one actually believes unless

given a grand tour via hands
cuffed to unbreakable plastic
behind the back pulled taut

no money no phone call no bail:
product for expenditure.
.or. process as prosecution

for the good of the people,
dante & duncan said. *the most
abused of an unrighteous order*

wrote the soledad brother.

{#289-128}

good people do not reside here—
screaming in a dark ocean

the body is not constitutional
  becomes more effective than
yelling this setup ain't right!

: THE MAKING OF {#289-128} IN FIVE PARTS

*

you will be arrested & sequestered
as property of the state as {#289-128}
   a beetle
   in a darlingtonia
might be more accurate.

*

each day/month/year builds to a question
 the response known before the query
again   & again
    disbelief is futile
on rehabilitation
you wait & . . .   wait—

*

at some point repetition sets in:
 boiled egg, farina, white bread, bland coffee
for breakfast reminders
of what   you have become {#289-128}
a nonbeing from which
escape or release is a fairytale.

*

the rec yard never alters its landscape:
dirt track, hoops, weight pit, fisticuffs—

*

the changing same . . . ?

8

: SORRY THIS NOT THAT POEM

raised block flower & plant bed.
 peonies, gardenias, poinsettias
plus a yellow orb slow rising
 over an endless golden scape—

darting through uncluttered space
 cardinals, thrashers, sparrows
blue air fragrant with lavender
 washing brain matter into virtue.

if only i could pastel alphabets
 onto a canvas of thistledown
yes, deceit comes to mind—
 .a lie. traitor. turncoat. recreant

backstabber here i would be
 gut shanked a million times.
this is not that poem nor am i
 that poet to hold your hand

.or. erase knothole screams
 blood on a cement floor .or.
suicide is another form of escape
 no-no-no—yes-i-do promise

the evil-ugly humans inflict
 on each other to their [selves]
how time is malice is death
 inflaming pupils with spite

inextinguishable if set free—
 forgive state poet {#289-128}
for not scribbling illusions
 of trickery as if timeless hell

could be captured by stanzas
 alliteration or slant rhyme—

: RHETORICAL, PERHAPS

we do not experience movement
  the cell a setting a chronic theme
we do not experience only exist

in the frame behind the cell we stand
  each step in place with the next still
standing we do not move until told

this instant we only have moments
  mementos relived in slow motion
a cinematic dream i see [you] the good

while [we] evildoers rot like pomegranate
  once sweet, fresh & vibrant—
rehabilitation is love letters to a ghost

discourse in the dayroom we look at
  the world on tv to see our false selves
inside a constructed frame until told

we enter as if we never left—

: .OR. THIS *MALUS* THING NEVER TO BE CONFUSED WITH JUSTICE

nothing symbolic. okay. dark is dark—
cage is cage. hunted & hunter are both

in the literal. make believe & *what ifs*
do not exist: a lie. nothing cryptic here.

okay. rape is rape. prey must pray. no
minute in the future safe from quiet

insertions of a shank in masking tape.
okay. nothing here infinite: only time

is constant to the merciful & merciless—
there are no allegories to hide behind.

he slit his wrists means he slit his fuckin wrists

okay? there is a cell with one window
just before day. dawn's early demise

magnifies a dull metal toilet. the cool
water cooling two can sodas. each

wall a slab of soft gray cinderblock, no
posters featuring eroticized women

with an exclusive in BLACK TAIL. okay.
the wall that slits the light does not

reveal nothing new, ever. the exposé
the changing same: always a holding.

one window offers a gateway. my face
pressed against the window & time

rules this empire. okay. the mind held
hostage by time. mind & body

conjoined twins. the other wall holds
a frame. the frame holds a metal door

to contain utter disbelief. of the visible:
walls are gray not like summer

but darker—*yes. there is darkness.* okay?

: ESCORTING THE CRIMINAL JUSTICE ADVOCATE THROUGH STATE PRISON

of being not alive but trapped—
in perpetual madness at roxbury
walk with trustee {#289-128} escorted

through habitual routines & storylines
a different kind of nightmare: life
for not taking life. one hour a day

under the feet at rec gravel crunches
around an oval track. for a decade
breathe deep the pollen & horse shit—

glorious oh the hills of hagerstown!
on the top tier watch angel jump
minus his wings & halo lifeless on impact—

a story of survival no one survives.
day after day become a callous heart
.or. a broken mind unable to escape—

frozen & hollowed there is no escaping
tonight. visit each unit after lock in—
taste the fetid air. cell by fucking cell

make no mistake language matters
through narration. mouth j-u-s-t-i-c-e
a filthy word in eyes of confined men.

{#289-128}

14

evolve toward the difficult thesis—
.a thing for sure, underscored at best.

: COUNTERPRODUCTIVE DEFINITIONS

(for those branded with

sentenced as lawless without a discharge
of course. immoral seems more valid
the con is the conviction itself. a trickster

for defendants. who without sin is a juror
in the mirror: a judge on the bench a d.a.
mimetic clones for the *good* of the people—

declared guilty by those with guilt. a decree
within a paradox of secretive legal secrets—
both sign & symbol with a felonious label

but meant as lifelong after the debt is paid—
who could be though not deemed corrupt.
in a state within the [state]ment. sanctions

with the ex can-not-never-be a smart thing.
label made legend by the original colonials—

WITHIN THE CRIMINAL JUSTICE SYSTEM (1)

the stain of incarceration)

assign to bad people but not. limited—
or: this *malus* thing in caged habitat,
a shady character. a cruel misnomer

to say the least; yet, ordinary people
are cruel. of uncertain ethical character—
good should be a criterion not a record

from medieval latin the evildoers: *fello*
a delinquent. though not exactly illegal—
or: the greatest lie ever told as stigma

wading as dead weight in quicksand.
all is never forgiven for the classified
obviously without expiration, a fate

some say. loser or lifer; yet, what is lost:
the evil the high-minded do. in the open—

: NOTHING AS IT SEEMS

minutes trickle to the slow hours. hours
   multiply toward a release date: *five*
plus three back up contemplated at night
   makes a court order meticulous. count

at count time creates habit, habitual. waiting
   on miracles means wait on baby jeezus—

here at roxbury correctional *eight years* stops
   short of a dime with a nickel done
creating another kind of normal

[outside's razor fence could be a gateway
   the housing unit emblematic of the morally good]

juvenile tried as a bonafide adult questions
   authority quite nice & by magic disappears
returning a broken boy beyond repair.

call it far-fetched or unreliable narrator
   they will say *we the key holders are god*
& [we] *are the servants of time created*—

an elaborate tale sentencing weaves, what
   gets lost in a brick cell: character, location
protagonist existing in dark matter:

a hollowed out echo chronicles truth. a man

stabbed in real time screams truth, truth
doesn't exist in a courtroom. for convicts
they will say: *he didn't see what he saw—*

: UNRELIABLE NARRATOR

distractions ring apparent:
gate, iron, cement, gun, dog,

division by categorization—
race is a factor manipulated

because you cannot depend
on distracted recall inside

delusions of the incarcerated—
this may be make-believe now:

a row of cells contain america's
war on drugs, the carnage

invisible within a ten-year bid—
brought in by corrections

from baltimore bundles of boy
.or. opioids for the uninformed—

hung out to dry while hanging
in the streets for black bodies:

—prison prescribed as cure—
blame shackles for diversions

for the system goes blameless:
cop, warden, d.a., politician

all cry necessity, a must, a need—
this is the fantastical dreamed up

in the mind of someone real.

: ROXBURY CORRECTIONAL BOOK CLUB

I. POETRY

AMERICAN JOURNAL arrives in a library cart
  dog-eared to page 18 "the prisoner"
  as if to start here in medias res, dear
  hayden: the [I] in me no longer lives

it vanished i confess the collective (we)
  is no better; yes, walls here are gray
  not green but know your poems sing—
  again, [I] does not exist, comrade. i do

between life & death in this infinite space
  with no clock no marker of time no
  calendars to ~~strike~~ out the day or days
  running together after lock in. i write—

the legal pad fills itself with regret
  [*ownership is mine even in this cage*]
  a brokenness dictated by time's torture:
  writs, habeas corpus, motions denied

in a house lacking doorknobs to turn, yes
  the cockroach caught became a pet
  at xmas my cellie snorted white lines
  to escape physical torture of the mind

cascading in & on itself rapid then slow—
  a program of abstinence & madness.

{#289-128}

II. MEMOIR (FOR OLD SKOOL)

gloved fist, flashlight, baton is fair.
  entering the hole requires protocol:

ears, mouth, gums, arms, lift & reach
  bend over, spread each butt cheek,

behold the steel holding cage that kills—
  a metal mirror bolted to cinderblock

old skool stares at the refracted image,
  age a natural antagonist of the young—

forgotten brown face a little boy once
  someone knew well decades before

life before puberty before adulthood
  every two years hair turns grayer—

a nickel gone with no redemption song
  he will never know if change is real:

computer shop, religion, g.e.d., college
  certificates, advocates, a degree

none changed THE QUALITY OF HURT—
  old skool is in the frame struggling

on good days he reads chester himes'
words corroborating street heroics

how else to define anecdotes of realism
or the slow fatality of imprisonment—

the sun cannot bear witness anymore
forget rope, lethal injection, or gunshot.

{#289-128}

III. FICTION

half-wet the cigarette half-lit a bugler
  rolled up outside walking to chow—
a fine mist picturesque & primeval

almost halfway until rain implodes
  into baptismal for sinners so believe
in uniform guards lining the walkway—

THE RESIDUE YEARS on loan from cell 2
  came last night the paperback version
bringing characters like champ here, inside—

a fool's dream .or. setup by subtraction
  too many pleas, illegal searches, guilty
at the thought of life though innocent

as the mirrored shaded bureaucrats—
  dreaming family i draw: wife-kid-dog
in my head time measures mathematics

that failed to reduce mandate to logic
  hidden in cells disguised as change—
the housing unit is an american critique

on full display cloaked in numb silence—
  there are no empty skeletons on wheels
with limbs pulled apart by a team of horses

the body is now instrument & tonight
a book might save my life after lock in—

IV. DRAMA

anything can be destroyed. for the skeptics trust
    donnie was deflowered one night after count time—
clearly this structure is obsolete says angela davis

& i sit in darkness expected to write about injustice,
    a witness to nothing on the stand but in op-eds
i can be quite believable with the unimaginable—

a report from cell 23, irony or ironical: i say truth
    on what plainly is a corrupt condition. identical
to the blueprint overlooked within the penal frame

you can't see: the backdraft's flashpoint a raging fire—
    this suicide must be. i must commit to killing the [I]
in order to save my[self] there is no hope for the flower.

under the bolted metal door it appears some days
    one act at a time. SHORT EYES the dramatic play slid
on cold cement, from cell to cell poet miguel piñero

is one of a few—who ever gave us prisoners, us—i write:
    [*society inverted*. imagine that concept. *color too*
this violation as only a beginning of what you knew]

come sit in the political madness alongside the bad,
    perception versus the real occurs quick,   .or.
.of course. crimes against donnie occur frequent—

27

: HOW TO BECOME THE INVISIBLE MAN

names must be on the list
    but no one will visit today

including children over 12.
    friends dissipated first

at roxbury weekdays are fixed:
    10-11 a.m. & 12 to 2:30 p.m.

weekends depend on an inmate's #—
    from d.c. take I-270 north

though the cutoff time stays at 2
    a visit might be miraculous.

.but. drive far-far west—get off
    (as if someone actually might)

at the sharpsburg exit (rt. 65)—
    since girlfriend never wrote

she will not proceed one mile
    or approach any access road.

after the transfer from county
    contemplate loneliness & why

family blocked every collect call—
    please follow the signs

believe a whole body can vanish.

{#289-128}

: QUIET BEFORE THE STORM IN THE DAYROOM

stainless steel tables with stop sign seats
  hold dominoes, checkers, playing cards
alongside a group of old heads studying

not the bible but the qur'an for balance.
  rippling keys from a manual typewriter
echo from cell 42 on the top tier—filing

a writ, perhaps a hail mary; yet, hope—
  in the dayroom men craft greeting cards
or bracelets from slivers of colored plastic

under the bolted tv big pun gets a tattoo
  the cost: five cup-a-soups & two kippers
for a naked lady drawn with a walkman

tricked out by a needle the cassette gone
  the music gone. hear the clank of metal
or thud from a steady stream of urine

in toilet water before the flush & release—
  there is laughter over our sadness
lingering beneath fake smiles someone

owes for a bag of heroin & before lock in
  will battle the creditor like a gladiator:
a spectacle we call theater of the absurd.

: WHEN BULLETS MISS BUT MEMORY LIVES

lost between freedom & restraint
a thing, an object innately resistant

to containment, containing that which
sucks living from the mind each day

metallic reflections reveal dull. dullness
distorted. the reflection a cell. a kinda

social order. skewing dreams & *damn*
before the trigger-squeeze the .44 was god

more addictive than china white. power was
three bullets shattering one windshield

a slumped figure in the passenger seat
delicately composed between day & night.

old heads say imagination kills though
in prison any one of these can be savior:

toothbrush, single-blade razor, metal spoon,
necessities for breathing. also respect

of religion, phone calls, dope debt & jive
lovers, mail call, visiting days, rec time,

another man's lie, another man's belief
blocked by a fence, a border—barbwire

circling the perimeter. even memories
  are nightmares alongside a five-year bid

how life without parole hung millimeters
  from the kidney, the aorta, the achilles,

bullets missing a whole contorted body,
  every refracted flashback a guilty recap

of the past, of a future that coulda been
  another judicial sentence altogether.

: COUNTERPRODUCTIVE DEFINITIONS

(for those branded with

trapped within a carceral state a bird—
a person or thing but mostly a thing
involuntary held under restraint &—

almost always restricted to a 6 by 9—
derivative of prison or *pre(hē)nsiōn*
from old french *prisonier* is a detainee

colored or a gender. given a namesake
used to be called indentured or slave
living in detainment unable to escape—

caught in a revolving door without exit
stamped with names often inaccurate—
relegated not necessarily to four walls

could be urban also from rural districts.
held in a frame. an idea as conceptual—

WITHIN THE CRIMINAL JUSTICE SYSTEM (2)

the stain of incarceration)

unable to resurrect from burnt ashes—
into confinement. humans chained up
doing a bid in the house of corrections.

medieval as usual. in context. outdated
punitive punishment. a constricted group
on eternal lock. behind bars. *incarceratus*

or: set up under lock & key. a whole body—
examining closer reveals how to define
another word for catalog-the-chattel—

tagged for deletion as habitual habit
a birthmark growing bigger over time
is of no consequence. to the sequestered:

could be a split. life doesn't matter at all
much bigger than THE NEW JIM CROW—

{#289-128}

POET-IN-RESIDENCE (CELL 23)

We are ourselves both the instrument of discovery and the instrument of definition.

—Charles Olson

: ON REFLECTION

because a box is a box humans are cultivated
into said box without choice or explanation, specimens
only existing—as in: (you—i—us). frame & flesh—
confined bone matter comprising a box reluctant
not to be a box. but nurtured inside the box, let's say
form which is shaped by & indigenous to the box &
the creator of the holy box—only leading to another
question about, of course, the infamous box—form
turns devious inside the box like any[thing] caged,
leaning to a non-empathetic approach steeped in revolt
—is judas in waiting. note: the box is not universal
nor the universal. whatever hope of otherworldliness
lies in the box itself. the box will not elongate, dissolve
or vanish without reaction to an action & here within
lies problems of perspective as in—there is none—zero.
along time's continuum, color, too, is encouraged
for the sake of the construction of the box, which
is precious as flickering light, but cannot be verified since
darkness is the original concept of all things human.

: AESTHETIC BEAUTY I REMEMBER I THINK

was that you we saw in our tainted conscience that peripheral place
a forgettable moniker at & beyond the edge to say you were there
out of reach would well be a slippage & even tho it appears as if
one aesthetic borderlines another in danger of being boundaried
you as in pristinely you were stowed away in that place that isn't—
a place more than vision could see: to touch to try became taboo
your category ungovernable & radical & illegal like someone said
this mode of communication we string together it doesn't equal
(us)—& you *oh-so-crazy*—blinded by time the same tawny fields
the flowing manmade streams: we bought into conscripted ideals
in that place whose name is merely a phantom of dead letters
the landmarks daily changing as if to get lost to find our way back
to nowhere & understand in a thousand standing mirrors a body
memorializes & nothing can erase what we saw the real you
in one fleeting moment as the day before & almost the day after
will never construct itself again this omen we had to keep asking
ourselves over & over the simplicity of an act: the casual step-aside
& the first minute of a new day   there you were—knowing

all we had to do was   leap—:

{#289-128}

: PHOTOGRAPH OF MY GIRL WINTER ON 135TH & BROADWAY TAPED TO THE WALL

in winter's negative cityscape
  pigeon shit remains obscured

behind a throng of urban dwellers.
  maybe these humans daydreamt
              (too hard
to speculate) in this polaroid
  each random stiff's objective

unknown. are names important
  i think not. i imagine the street vendor
                  (on broadway
saying into a korean woman's ear
  might rain today buy umbrella)

perpendicular to this arbitrary act—
  two men hug at the subway station
                  (forever
love withers against the incoming train
  amidst pedestrians). i can tell
                  (winter aged
fast with each vanished season)
  the transformed block on display

within this minuscule snapshot—
  the city once known now gone.

: IN A DREAM THE SILENT

slashes through my eyes quick: sunlight
   & a logician's puzzle tells me i am in a cell

seeing what i am seeing. this vision i keep
   waking to, among trees, the dead static

in my ear, a blue-gray sky over the archaic
   carriage house, a shadow floating hung

alongside rain clouds ready to unleash
   the pictorial: a woman this time. pleated

into sunflowers. against which horizon she
   openly lies indifferent. on pristine grass

with the horizon parallel, inside the woman
   screaming up at high noon & way beyond

is a ventriloquist's voice trapped. *h-e-l-p m-e*
   echoes the valley, a mute scream it is,

crepe myrtle trees sing soft this brittle night,
   every branch tip wind-whistling softly

over the mountaintop, the ardent wind blows
   in my dream: *the voiceless are alive, too—*

{#289-128}

: BUT SHE WASN'T FROM MY GEOGRAPHICAL LOCATION

i've been trying to recall nostalgia, how
hidden within deep memory they call it

saudade, its origin portugal. i've never been
lost to a lover, sadly misled, discarded,

all the ache inside me caged—yes, i lie
between the triangle of yr paradoxical

sweet melancholy, eradicated & saddened
something vibrates this pulse, maybe

the guitar i once coveted which twanged
all night long. totally perplexed am i

an unbreakable will searching continuous
for that shudder left in me. forever gone

yr ghost of fatalistic moans circle my head
again & again. i can't lie—of course, i wait

shipwrecked, my portuguese love i drown
into the mythology of you & linger still.

: DEAR ETHERIDGE (2)

because i am older now i can reflect on
that mystical spring of my 17th year

under the spell of love, how rage electric
shocked this juvenile body: frizzled

veins singed with desire. in her heart
a syntax unspoken. we swam clueless

no compass to guide what we thought
lasts forever, but nothing lasts forever.

one day in the future i would scatter,
reminded of that kinetic body haunted

by what never was. a foundation—a promise
of eternity: our longing created chaos

& togetherness became a brine we loathed
to taste. liquor always fails to obliterate

before the first cup of coffee, what i knew.
& every morning i holla *man down*

man down, drowning in my echo.

: ABRACADABRA

long before you knew
  something changed inside

you became icicle cold
  as if what lay before us

you saw the road to nowhere
  winding through our hearts

the lump in your throat
  before you left, yes you forecasted

each lie we would eventually speak
  when you said *i'm out*

& i split, too, even before
  we made love disappear—

: TROUBLE THE WATER

across the pockmarked street through the breezeway, around the
way of no-way-at-all—

the bridge, real & imagined be troubled water overground. don't
trouble the concept but we did. on the one looking for the two, or
2 for 1 in certain geographical locations unerases the erased.

the get back up beat do it again—freedom ain't nothing not even
a word. so don't give me that regurgitated sound reprogrammed.
an unconditional condition is what we asked for someone
yelled—*our ass is what we follow*—then all light begins
as dark matter—b.a.m.—forever is what you want it to be.
　　　　.word up.

: WHEN THE GOVERNMENT DOESN'T LOVE YOU (THE EIGHTIES)

seagulls punctuate morning with a cry,
encrypted shrieks reveal a troubled state.
bright bands of silver linger beneath gray
guiding rudderless humans from shelter
to soup kitchen, & then the labor pools:
daily work, daily pay. equates: a meal
a 40 oz. & crack rock. at ground zero
proletariats suffer at length the residuals
of a city at war: neighborhoods saturated
with unlearned chemists, a nation trying
to erase a *nation* in the subconscious. first:
disappear the self (collectively), infiltrate
from within, poison one drop per body:
carlos, short-tee, donnell, bay-boy. take,
complicate their adolescence with promise
(gone). second: cut the head, & the body,
in all its beautiful contradictions, falls—
baby create baby & raise baby. the cycle—
somewhere in the caribbean a plane loads
brick by brick, a death house. slaves
made every day. addicts begetting addicts—

: OPEN AIR MARKET ON HERKIMER & NOSTRAND, BROOKLYN (1989)

at the end of a tumultuous decade
sequestered in a bad b movie. soldiers

line antagonistic sidewalks, dedicated
to a lifelong commitment with a bag

full of baggies. too many block-boys
to mention marketing their brand

of hook line & sinker: death straight
through a glass shooter. in the open

single file, addicts arrive starry-eyed
with dollar bills, coins—ghost

memories of ornate smoke. triple beam
mathematics will balance each fate—

shadows are their faces who look upon
the kid, no more than twelve & a gun

tucked waist level at the ready. he not
alone as each protagonist packs armor

their mother couldn't give them, love
a postscript, the tenement building

held hostage by a pipeline from bogotá
to the big apple: a primal scene.

{#289-128}

: 1990 (A FORECAST)

at 5 am, a throng of sunken eye sockets—the ones
tweaking, through a square windowpane, emerge
—*who will save fanon's wretched* mutters a single man

five stories up in a heights studio, the outside brutal
lamplight beaconing thirst for crack, for escape
the outlined spectacle muted below. for clarification

no noise, a muted shuffle, no change ever. time
changes the historical always. at dawn 20 years later
this single man will speak lovingly of sight, recalling

as time permits gray haze over the city, lost humans
redacted, out of which sparked countless storylines
& chaos birthing prisons. but in the glass pane

five stories up in a heights studio, the single man awaits
glaucoma's night blanket, & yet a witness to ruin
20 years later, homeless voice on the corner, he will be—

: SEX WORKERS ON SMOKE BREAK 1994

five stories high winding back stairwells
tell the story: gia & koko knife a cigar,

a silver scalpel runs under the belly's surface,
tobacco spilling onto steps like placid blood

not on a gurney alongside redcap plastic vials,
cracked glass, used condoms, dirty needles.

gia flashes back to *oh-my-god*—the perp
violated without say-so: occupational hazard?

perhaps. perhaps street life nurtures ruin,
horror, post-traumatic stress, combat

zones squared to ten block radiuses. both ladies
time themselves out with a whoolie to medicate—

illegal & yes, not a doctor but koko skillfully
scrapes the guts, inserts weed & crack, licks

not sews the leaf tight, thinking: *it's crazy
seven days a week, three-sixty-five.* diagnosis:

a fucking jungle. the lighter's flick triggers
flame: two shadows dance, almost airless

outlines, inside their recall regrets of flesh
giving the milk for free, the damage done—

{#289-128}

: WHEN YOUR SILENCE WILL NOT SAVE YOU

in the aftermath you remember the fist
  upside her head. did you see. saying *no*
almost instinctively, you say *no* again.

you remember no audio with the beating
  to follow in the alley. you remember
clearly not thinking. the woman got beat

from the other side of the street. imagine
  you witnessed her (walker of the night)
illusion to fantasy built up. in your head

the after-scream. in the alley she could be
  dead. you thought *no one will remember*
the freeze-frame each night whispering

in cell 23 at night: *you coulda saved me . . .*

: IMAGINATION RUNNING WILD —

in the dream fabric of one's [cell]
    dangling from c tier, if not bodies,

leaves fluttering against night's rustic
    sound: a chinook, a brittle *swoosh*—

down by the riverbed. call it virginal
    alongside open-field: day & then

that frame: a cold shivering human

on the block one heel gutter bound.
    secreted inside a storefront's cleft

a person drowned by gin's delirium

suspended inside a half-pint
    copped with loose change. say a [self] less

figure in a scream, another deferral

sleepwalking wide-awake above
    daffodil heads painted alabaster—

but what of the purple wisteria's blue,

the mockingbird's obbligato—
    altering time if for a moment. if

{#289-128}

50

a raven is stuck in obscure dark

of night: here everything returns
   into another mute corridor &—

: BLACK MALE PRIVILEGE

an orange horizon beyond the sunset—
it could've been like that but it wasn't.

again he ran like trained to run, again
quiet into the low brush almost noon

because he ran, the coloring of an ahistorical
3D fright through the barrel's scope

but it could have been a day like today,
swans skimming the lake's smooth surface—

early american nothing but comedy,
who knows nothing of death, of life,

only a boy or manchild or bogeyman—

: BEFORE THE BEAUTY .OR. HOW COULD U FORGET?

locate the nearest overlooked neighborhood—
   extract all humans restrained underneath
life's bootheel. replace with millennials coddling

postcolonial guilt, but not. ignore the woman's
   cardboard [HELP] tattered, stained & broken
like her: imagine being long-ago unseen, erased

in between the throng, existing as nonentity. ask
   too, if gun be instrument what chord whizzed
amid crestfallen shadows mute lingering in limbo

a decade. go from a to z listing the dead: too many
   to name, but try: twan, bird, fella, delante . . .
no deader now than the moment of collision—

cold steel & shots fired—death, what did we know
   of dying? don't forget a love strangling addicts
caught in a docetic whirlwind with no blue sail.

before the corner becomes distorted remember:
   one more time inhale memory deep to include:
the bad & terrible beauty just beneath the living.

{#289-128}

P<small>OET IN</small> N<small>EW</small> Y<small>ORK</small>

I just don't want them to pigeonhole me. I feel
they are trying to chain me down.
—Federico García Lorca
(trans. Greg Simon & Stephen White)

: REMEMBER

do not turn from the difficult thesis—
  think back to the slim praying man
in cell 15 with needle stuck in vein
  religion nor dope can stop time—

remember 72 in a unit built for 30
  that never-ending revolving door
  —or the overcrowded choir singing—
  I am THE WRETCHED OF THE EARTH

typed on a smith-corona at night
  how cell 23 demanded rabbled art—
what about the couple in cell 22
  lifers who found love doing a bid—

father & son as cellies on the top tier
  no generation will be left behind—
too many bodies lingering in limbo
  the worn out illusion of truth see—

memorialize faces you will forget—
  victim turned perpetrator in cell 6
sold at age 8 for a bag of meth
  nothing is black & white—

: {#289-128} — STILL INVISIBLE, TOO

after the Invisible Man statue on the Upper West Side
(for the fallen ones & those still to fall)

a stone's hurl from the henry hudson
   riverside converges into 150th street
foundationing a bronze cutout man
   his metal insides hollow, erased
midstride in a hurried stroll, as if
   running from the police is a trope
cyclic within time's continuum.
   high above ground level stereotype's
exhibit A in medias res defines it[self]—
   tonight's moon illuminates the dark
docile hudson. across the g.w. bridge
   car beams stab through late traffic
& onto a park bench i, {#289-128}, sit
   while observing this troubled man
more me, a mimetic confused clone
   of trauma, temporal space, history
caught in color construction, & if
   literature reflects human existence,
ellison nailed the novel, as in people
   refuse to see the who of what i am
since before post-racial. i am labeled:
   armed, dangerous, known to pack,
dark & hyphenated, the typecast
   memorialized in perpetual fear. time

{#289-128}

never ticks, the clock forever strikes
  midnight & high noon together.
tonight i must confess skin color
  is a race that never stops running—

: A PRIMER FOR SURVIVING A TRAFFIC STOP

if seated in car remain calm.
pull over. position hands
at eleven & three, assume
this will not go okay. recall
brown, bell, martin, a trail
of blood. ignore the raven
hovering the rooftop. it's not
a matter of respect, speech
or liberty, & yes, understand
survival be right now, if you
survive. swallow that pride
it can ignite swift death—
replay the past slow: unarmed
man shot with hands high
.or. police chokehold too strong
again, ignore the raven & recognize
you the invisible *thing-being*,
a bogeyman, a proletariat
open season means you, baby boy—
the target minimized into
a circling bull's-eye—you
this not a game nor test—
sadly, you the game. facts
will be misremembered: he
lunged, appeared to have—
a bulge, dressed wrong,
reached. a large metal object—
the raven hovering wants

your death. but fuck that,
breathe deep & prepare
for the figure approaching—

: AMERICANS IN TIMES SQUARE

mid-atlantic but further northeast:

—underground the #1 breaches
dark matter: above dwellers
meander with perceived purpose—

a double-decker slow drags 42nd
each bottom pane collaborating
varied accounts of jean & jim—

amos & aretha also are present—
equal within the glass's echo

{#289-128}

a little girl on the sidewalk
pleads for cotton candy
no sweets replies her pop—

sergio from inwood is plastered
wandering aimless with lolita's
goodbye offered last night—

collapsed on cardboard draped
in archaic news not rainbows
a mother assures 3 offspring

he will never come back to us—
giving voice to the [un]scene
nobody notices the [un]seen:

a museum of american ruin
.or. the silent stream of dialogue
of: *do you have any change?*—

: ON THE HUDSON RIVER AT PIERS PARK

3 quarters of a mile in girth a placid watercourse
almost marine blue but more silver under the sun
on manhattanville's shoreline. a self-contained break
right between morningside & washington heights
uncovers three sets of benches facing east, three west—
2 white carolina skiffs sputter up current against
a noon tide. several meters away inland: LOOK OUT
FOR NUMBER ONE looms overhead on a billboard
the actual #1 train 2 blocks parallel to the sign. 14 black
lampposts with filament light provide 7 freeze-frames
into new jersey on the island's west side at piers park.
(we) meditate by a bucolic beach stonewashed clean
the pristine harlem cove & hudson cliffs vanished long ago—
the italian neighborhoods the language lost. wind
against the face & one egret suspends like a guillotine blade
in time watching (us) the landscape the millennials
who soon will be an idea in the theory of man too
replaced by generation z. an unforgiving continuum—

{#289-128}

64

: RIVERSIDE DRIVE STATE PARK

BECAUSE 3AM IS THE PERFECT
TIME TO LOOK
FOR THAT MANUSCRIPT

the billboard reads, {#289-128}
composes verse by riverside drive
on a concrete barricade

bracing the curved walkway
up to riverbank state park—
ROUTE 9A too holds the sign

DON'T TRUST THE CLOUDS
south by southwest
white wakes behind the lone trawler

sans the wind on the hudson
trails a san agustín replica.
a ball double bounces, *you can't*

check me, the girl giggles—
dressed in camouflage a boy
rides an immaculate bike,

spokes gleaming against the sun—
only trees with dead branches
miss the soft breeze. as always

earplugs hang from walkers
walking up the walkway absent
what {#289-128} is witness to.

{#289-128}

: RANDY WESTON'S AFRICAN RHYTHMS CONCERT, THE DAY AFTER

(FOR SALLY ANN HARD & ALEX BLAKE)

as if, the wall behind
    was not a wall
harper pretended

JAZZ STANDARD the sign
    did not exist, as if
miles said *play what*

you don't know, on key
    weston responded
not with breath

but breath's imagination—
    in the train car sally-ann
daydreams last night,

this paradox, we live in
    structures. she believes
somebody forget to tell

blake don't go; yet, he did
    on upright bass, left
her an aesthetic mess

this morning on the #1—

: BEWARE OF THE BANDLEADER

what if all notes composed
sung out only to be sung
                reinvented
again   in form
            but still
   (re)stated as sound—

against the [state] & what if all notes sung
failed miserably, as such

      to listen, to re-sound as if
      a note sung not a "thing."

& what if no one said a metaphor
about plastic prophets   who
   lullaby us to sleep

pulling night's slow hum,
& what if that note sang—

                    *

at a lone lamplight a clone
in whiteface is singing like a clown

      a flawed love note—
      trees bend toward the want of it,
leaning back   i can't
catch the sway of the fool's pendulum—

after & beyond the hudson
along the rain splattered pier.
& walking away i felt empty,

                              still
going back we tried to reconcile when
damn
          another safe note
—& boy, real tears i cried: *what if that*
became your bandleader to the world—
                          see
    somebody changing
    the sound (i thought

& it aint the changing same,
    man), yes—

: ARS POETICA (3): STAY WOKE

faking the blues for a hand clap—
feel good moment for sake of self

glowing with laziness—shortcut
to the long game, a social media

internet sensation as in "liking"
not never wanting to be a color

until award season roll 'round.
contrived, unreal—an imaginary

perpetual love for the afro-pick—
stealing away only to be co-opted

as the lone kid with all the toys
nobody wanna play with, a lie

presented as truth as american reel
edited, monochromatic, a filtered

fashionable desire—nurtured
within the stomach of the beast

most fear; they, or. specifically—
the associated do walk among us

living an [un]state by the [state]
programmed as intelligentsia elite—

{#289-128}

: SUBWAY CHRONICLES

I. FLASHBACK TO THE CELL

the last stop is also a beginning point
  on the c at 168th POETRY IS HARD
catches my eye before we depart
  against the reflecting neon signs
as square tiles parallel lives lived
  in a box or cell—we alone the man
& [I] of no significance until he exits—
  the grinding wheels pull away
from 155th—a ghost compartment now
  analogous to time spent in solitary.
i occupied this same mute hush
  when white boy met his living shadow
in a split second on the cold concrete
  bringing to view faces pressed
inside rectangle glass—the aftersound
  resonates loud year after year—
(white boy died from the epistles of dear john)
  appearing at 125th a person is reading
THE ESSENTIAL ETHERIDGE KNIGHT
  on the train today no one reads
& we continue swathed in noise—

*II. ON THE A TO STATEN ISLAND (COURTESY OF THE RAPID
TRANSIT CONSTRUCTION COMPANY)*
for Gwendolyn Brooks

traveling parallel to the # 2
until we stop at 22nd
    catapults passengers
southbound to flatbush deeper
into tranquil dark matter

no one enters our car,
    we begin again. pass
spray-painted hieroglyphics
    over soiled crossties,
through black spat night

we a sliding shoe on the 3rd rail,
    600 volts, a whirlwind—
distinct lingua franca in the distant:
    italian, german, irish,
immigrant laborers
    sinking in quicksand at canal,
the life lost between
34ᵀᴴ & TIMES SQUARE,
the dream lost—

a *clack* lodges rail &
    we continue,

exiting at the last stop, we
board staten island ferry
   up the winding staircase
topside we go—
depart angling away from
brooklyn's bridge, we
port to liberty's statue—

III. A LESSON IN HUMANITY AFTER LEAVING THE
METROPOLITAN MUSEUM OF ART

having left the met's rooftop
overlooking central park east

awestruck by birches & blossoms
 at 86th we board the B
to brighton beach

downtown.
 a lady enters at 59th, razor slashes
denting her frail cheeks & begins:

i don't want to sell my body
for it is an instrument, her

pupils sing violent fury:
 gun against temple
knife perpendicular to throat—

help is the last pleading word
miss plaid skirt ignores
before exiting at TIMES SQUARE.

IV. TRANSFER

eight silver poles down the aisle
    a toddler hangs limp onto her mother—

doors close. a drone nonetheless carries
    for two minutes (us) in which time

an armenian commuter texts: [luv,
    forever can-NOT be defined]

beige pentagon tile. blue metal columns—
    the platform. arrival:

block numbers display 96TH. we
    exit to the film poster, the whiteface woman

featured prominent as backdrop, her
    black mane backwards, vertical

endorsing the film: THE QUIET ONES; yet,
    impending train brakes grind

against rail & stop. doors open. we begin
    uptown, east. next stop 110TH

blinks overhead. a nomadic figure
    materializes shouting over the p.a. system:

in another life your murdered self
be more alive than dead.

{#289-128}

V. LADY WITH THE WORN LEATHER JOURNAL ON THE #2

the curt jolt & stop of a 5-car set
  into the story. inserted her[self]
is what the jolt did, to the writer

what she imagines—god at play
  with denizens, pink unicorns
dying hollow inside a cave, here

the acoustic adjusts, then a lil loud
  rattle & shake around the corner.
stop. two people enter, two exit—

another jolt, she writes: dark river,
  seagulls piping incessantly. a tanker
100 yards out holds her image over-

head, tunnel lights blink—spine
  bent over the journal, sideways
her pencil perpendicular. stop.

each body a question, she writes
  class will be the death of culture,
my skull an instrument, she thinks

through a platform & over a bridge.

VI. *GIRL MODEL J ON EXHIBIT (POWER)*

*Margaret Bowland demands that our society acknowledge the
backstory that accompanies our national narratives, that we validate
the lives we attempt to erase and destroy.*

—Leola Dublin Macmillan

we exit at 23ᴿᴰ STREET. walk .5 miles & enter DRISCOLL |
    BABCOCK—
a white rectangle with 3 white columns rises from the floor,
aluminum pipes hang overhead. a spool of barbwire coiled
around each pole functions as a noose around an unsuspecting
black-brown or any *other* thing neck, but also, 6 ravens, 2 circle
each pole &, of course, a clandestine allegory trails the hidden
    skyline—
in this present display zoom closer & rose petals accenting
barbwire turn into dollar bills & capitalism, the oxymoron
that it is—can never be forgotten, the damage complete. & then,
too—we cannot stop the objectification, the innate ignorance
of gender & so J burns against the structure that constructed
the unafraid blue barrette   .or.   the gold heart locket dangling
from her ears. *freedom:* (us), yours & mine, i want to say. *they
failed us, too,* we never forget, *our construction & yours.* an
    eternal
footrace & the black raven perched on the white pole knows,
waits for the cockcrow of death, of self, to be complete. we know
    too—
the mechanization of the city, that glittering republic: failed.

{#289-128}

VII. GIRL MODEL J CONTINUED: IN BROOKLYN (DISTURBING THE PEACE)

mottled faces merge into one concept of human, even
if riders on the train are unaware, at the core, they are
the same—: a continuous drone of flesh. we've taken
this ride before, you & i, & it was (us). & now it is (us)
again, kinetically along time's continuum, defying
space, or how we be   .or.   sound. advancing forward
for the sake of the narrative let's reverse continuum
matter to a brownstone on a block of brownstones in
brooklyn, the recent (re)incarnation of GIRL MODEL J on
canvas & linen draped from the artist's redbrick wall.
J again is our divine nomadic protagonist & her
adolescent spine is to (us), but still she glances back
before walking toward a perceived "wonderland"
accented with glades, meadows & a never-ending
turquoise lake. pulling away from the station stop,
doors closing, the klieg light through the tunnel (here
& escaped), the evolution of GIRL MODEL J has been
remarkable. at 12, she is on the cusp of becoming a
young woman, & one can only contemplate if J
understands the significance of the symbolism within
her own frame. alongside the darkened tunnel, riding
the shake & rattle of the train is the image of J looking
over her shoulder at you, i, (us) as if it were (we) who
could grant permission to advance, to face an
uncertainty that consumes girls' lives at a young age.

VIII. *CLOWN LEAPS TWO STORIES INTO A BLACK HOLE FROM THE #1*

next to a clown in whiteface striped
    shadows penetrate a child's pupils
(re)living the arabesque, the *other*
    side-by-side, commuters compliant

to the train's drone—back to the clown
    opposite a lady reading sheet music—

we exit a tunnel: through a pane clouds
    break in—then out & there is indigo:
daylight if only for a moment.
    tenements bleeding against

summer's equinox, winding red fire escapes
    appear then don't before we descend—

back into the historical, the cerebral dark—
    exiting 125ᵀᴴ STREET outdoor platform
two stories up the transient clown leaps,
    passing (us) at ground zero into a hole,

    yelling *jump in to get out, be...*

{#289-128}

IX. THE SUBWAY & THE EX-

silence permeates the #5 train—
  JOIN THE REVOLUTION hangs over
the seated construction worker [gender
  is irrelevant] at barclays center

a flood of teenagers bombard
  quietness once absolute—
backstories aligned in the car
  never will be revealed unlike me

the forever felon the seated *ex-*
  afraid of a past without hope
on an island alone manhattan
  resembles a middle finger on the map

upside down birding the hudson—
  over the rails grinding halt
old ghost screech too loud
  night air laced with terror

memory in a cage haunts—
  one night after count time
afraid to shed tears—weakness
  tore flesh bit by bit then

someone yelled read dennis brutus's
  LETTERS TO MARTHA for context

another continent same theme—
at fulton street the kids exit

talking winter & summer homes
privilege knows no etiquette—
what revolution for {#289-128}?
is what i ask in silence.

{#289-128}

X. *AS IN, {#289-128} THE PROTAGONIST*

exiting darkness begins the process
 by which, of course, [I] dissolves

dim opaque, & a train whistling
 by the last window starboard.

against plate glass bubbled the cheek
 but then oblique, as in—

pressed ever so silly dumb the night
 vibrant & uptown folk trapped

in a maze of boundaries & books
 THE SOULS OF BLACK FOLK—or so

thinks our protagonist. no matter
 totally recuses itself from the living, it

begins dream as manifest destiny.
 there is departure in arrival

trapped in an impossible construct.
 say the construct walks upright

in search of freedom everywhere.

a historical fallacy willing the body.

say skin construction is black

deepening the scene's projection.
let's call {#289-128} human.

{#289-128}

: WALKING WITH GHOST IN HARLEM

the paperback entered through the slit
  MANCHILD IN THE PROMISED LAND at count time—
after bag & baggage one night in a bar
  all those images rush back over laughter
beneath a congregation of drunken voices—
  what did it mean walking with ghost
unseen to the nakedness dark demands.
  there is a scent lingering will not leave—
must stop the clanking inside won't stop—
  rottweilers jaw-jacking uninterrupted
in the yard on sunday. a circumference
  around the track again & one airplane
fighting cumulus clouds breaks free—
  chained to the past a corrective measure
looking for salvation in books i once wrote
  DOWN THESE MEAN STREETS saved me
& sonny within the esophagus of justice.
  about prison: the protagonist returns
through a windowless sunset a tragedy
  having seen skylines etched in haze—
there are walls pat behind this freedom
  undiscovered & yet too real each day
an electric fence around the neck echoes
  metal rattling long hours stretched
either way subject to a condition. a past
  a dagger through the heart cannot kill—

: ARS POETICA (1): ART AS PROPAGANDA

forget about revisionist history or the body.
say xenophobia. but say it backwards, now

plainly, to the holy ignant this be not a test
extract ignant from the alphabet take back

the illegal naming of things, take back natives
trying to love pilgrims pulled up by a helping hand:

take back murderers who invented whiteness.
i am not post or post-racial or post-human. i am

color-constructed {#289-128} & you can't take it back
i am melanin, & perhaps we have lost our minds.

some laws are cold bullshit & poems need to bite
spit venom, rebel-rouse. say muthafuck that:

rapid firing like machine guns into the absurd.
question: where is the baraka of this generation?

fuck a law, muthafuck the state, fuck beneficiaries
from plantations: okay say illegal now. perhaps

irony be a cold bitch, invert madness. rata-tat-
tap someone with love from a bullet who dares

to gain from privilege. say you must be crazy
while digging a good-foot out of somebody's ass.

: AFTER RUIN

beauty after ruin lingers on the *event* horizon: infinity
plus one, a new monin' echoing yesterday's cataclysm,
a confluence of aestheticisms climaxing into a new way
of looking—: in. ruin does this and perhaps is evermore
tied to the beautiful. in pursuit of beauty there is always
already a series of invisible vertical bars, the indented
metal shadows streaming across your face, reminders of
how you border yourself off, reduced to a subjugated
human in a cell. a human cannot divide its [self] into
fragments, it just is, but you can't just *be*, so you
become subject/object of your own ridicule. the figure
in the windowpane, chained to a way of seeing the [self],
a mirror of distorted noise, is a recorded memory
dictating an *event*, how the figure now bends the corner
(*event approaching*), pushing against memory (*event
past*), and what it produces: moments of reflection:
hanging from a tree, swinging maple leaves bodily
themselves against the moon's half lunar light onto the
glittering sound. language concurs through tremolo-
singing thrashers, stuck in suspended animation, staring
down into a sheet of pitch-dark blue. blowing like a flute,
the gentle wind is an echo of things to come, and the
afterimage of the figure(s) is that which will become,
again and again: {#289-128} a repeated action.

ACKNOWLEDGMENTS

Thank you to the editors of the following print and online publications in which these poems first appeared, some in different forms and under different titles.

"{#289-128} PROPERTY OF THE STATE: SORRY THIS NOT THAT POEM," "{#289-128} PROPERTY OF THE STATE: .OR. THIS *MALUS* THING NEVER TO BE CONFUSED WITH JUSTICE," and "{#289-128} POET-IN-RESIDENCE (CELL 17): BEFORE THE BEAUTY .OR. HOW COULD U FORGET?" first appeared in *Poetry* magazine.

"{#289-128} PROPERTY OF THE STATE: ROXBURY CORRECTIONAL BOOK CLUB" first appeared in the *Kenyon Review*.

"{#289-128} POET-IN-RESIDENCE (CELL 17): ON REFLECTION" first appeared in *PoetryNow*.

"{#289-128} POET-IN-RESIDENCE (CELL 17): BUT SHE WASN'T FROM MY GEOGRAPHICAL LOCATION" first appeared in *The Rumpus*.

"{#289-128} POET-IN-RESIDENCE (CELL 17): BLACK MALE PRIVILEGE" first appeared in *Gulf Coast*.

"{#289-128} POET IN NEW YORK: RANDY WESTON'S AFRICAN RHYTHMS CONCERT, THE DAY AFTER (FOR S. A. H.)" first appeared in the *Massachusetts Review*.

"{#289-128} POET IN NEW YORK: A PRIMER FOR SURVIVING A TRAFFIC STOP" first appeared in *CURA: A Literary Magazine of Art & Action*.

The selections "VI. *GIRL MODEL J ON EXHIBIT (POWER)*" and "VII. *GIRL MODEL J CONTINUED: IN BROOKLYN (DISTURBING THE PEACE),*" from the series "{#289-128} POET IN NEW YORK: SUBWAY CHRONICLES," first appeared in *Obsidian: Literature & Arts in the African Diaspora*.

Acknowledgments

THE UNIVERSITY PRESS OF KENTUCKY
NEW POETRY AND PROSE SERIES

This series features books of contemporary poetry and fiction that exhibit a profound attention to language, strong imagination, formal inventiveness, and awareness of one's literary roots.

SERIES EDITOR: Lisa Williams

ADVISORY BOARD: Camille Dungy, Rebecca Morgan Frank, Silas House, Davis McCombs, and Roger Reeves

Sponsored by Centre College